I WAS HERE...

THINGS YOU SHOULD
KNOW

I pray to see you again on the other
side when it's your time. So wipe
your tears...

My last wish...

Burial Arrangements preference

....

....

....

....

....

....

....

....

....

My last wish...

Burial Arrangements
preference

....

....

....

....

....

....

....

....

....

My last wish...

Burial Arrangements
preference

· ·

· ·

· ·

· ·

· ·

· ·

· ·

· ·

· ·

My last wish...

Burial Arrangements preference

....

....

....

....

....

....

....

....

....

My last wish...

Burial Arrangements preference

....

....

....

....

....

....

....

....

....

My last wish...

Burial Arrangements
preference: Hymnals

My last wish...

Burial Arrangements
preference: Hymnals

....

....

....

....

....

....

....

....

....

My last wish...

Burial Arrangements preference: Songs

· ·

· ·

· ·

· ·

· ·

· ·

· ·

· ·

· ·

My last wish...

Burial Arrangements
preference: Songs

. . . .

. . . .

. . . .

. . . .

. . . .

. . . .

. . . .

. . . .

My last wish...

Burial Arrangements
preference: Songs

My last wish...

Burial Arrangements preference: Songs

My last wish...

Burial Arrangements
preference: Bible Reading

My last wish...

Burial Arrangements
preference: Bible Reading

· ·

· ·

· ·

· ·

· ·

· ·

· ·

· ·

· ·

My Assets

ASSETS

My Assets

ASSETS

My Assets

ASSETS

INSURANCE COVER

INSURANCE COVER

INSURANCE COVER

INVESTMENTS

INVESTMENTS

INVESTMENTS

INVESTMENTS

INVESTMENTS

INVESTMENTS

INVESTMENTS

BANK ACCOUNT INFORMATION

BANK:

ACCOUNT NUMBER:

ACCOUNT OFFICER:

ACCOUNT OFFICER'S CONTACT:

ACCOUNT BALANCE:

BANK ACCOUNT INFORMATION

BANK:

ACCOUNT NUMBER:

ACCOUNT OFFICER:

ACCOUNT OFFICER'S CONTACT:

ACCOUNT BALANCE:

BANK ACCOUNT INFORMATION

BANK:

ACCOUNT NUMBER:

ACCOUNT OFFICER:

ACCOUNT OFFICER'S CONTACT:

ACCOUNT BALANCE:

BANK ACCOUNT INFORMATION

BANK:

ACCOUNT NUMBER:

ACCOUNT OFFICER:

ACCOUNT OFFICER'S CONTACT:

ACCOUNT BALANCE:

BANK ACCOUNT INFORMATION

BANK:

ACCOUNT NUMBER:

ACCOUNT OFFICER:

ACCOUNT OFFICER'S CONTACT:

ACCOUNT BALANCE:

DEBTORS

NAME:

AMOUNT:

DUE DATE:

PAYMENT TERMS AND
CONDITIONS:

DEBTORS

NAME:

AMOUNT:

DUE DATE:

PAYMENT TERMS AND
CONDITIONS:

DEBTORS

NAME:

AMOUNT:

DUE DATE:

PAYMENT TERMS AND
CONDITIONS:

DEBTORS

NAME:

AMOUNT:

DUE DATE:

PAYMENT TERMS AND
CONDITIONS:

DEBTORS

NAME:

AMOUNT:

DUE DATE:

PAYMENT TERMS AND
CONDITIONS:

DEBTORS

NAME:

AMOUNT:

DUE DATE:

PAYMENT TERMS AND
CONDITIONS:

CREDITORS

NAME:

AMOUNT:

DUE DATE:

PAYMENT TERMS AND
CONDITIONS:

OTHER IMPORTANT THINGS TO NOTE

SOCIAL MEDIA ACCOUNT:

PASSWORD

SOCIAL MEDIA ACCOUNT:

PASSWORD

OTHER IMPORTANT THINGS TO NOTE

SOCIAL MEDIA ACCOUNT:

PASSWORD

SOCIAL MEDIA ACCOUNT:

PASSWORD

OTHER IMPORTANT THINGS TO NOTE

OTHER IMPORTANT THINGS TO NOTE

OTHER IMPORTANT THINGS TO NOTE

OTHER IMPORTANT THINGS TO NOTE

OTHER IMPORTANT THINGS TO NOTE

OTHER IMPORTANT THINGS TO NOTE

OTHER IMPORTANT THINGS TO NOTE

OTHER IMPORTANT THINGS TO NOTE

OTHER IMPORTANT THINGS TO NOTE

____

____

____

____

____

____

____

____

OTHER IMPORTANT THINGS TO NOTE

OTHER IMPORTANT THINGS TO NOTE

OTHER IMPORTANT THINGS TO NOTE

OTHER IMPORTANT THINGS TO NOTE

OTHER IMPORTANT THINGS TO NOTE

OTHER IMPORTANT THINGS TO NOTE

OTHER IMPORTANT THINGS TO NOTE

OTHER IMPORTANT THINGS TO NOTE

OTHER IMPORTANT THINGS TO NOTE

OTHER IMPORTANT THINGS TO NOTE

www.ingramcontent.com/pod-product-compliance
Lightning Source LLC
Chambersburg PA
CBHW072126150726
47999CB00005B/2150